D0761980

Classic Marques

MUSTANG

Classic Marques

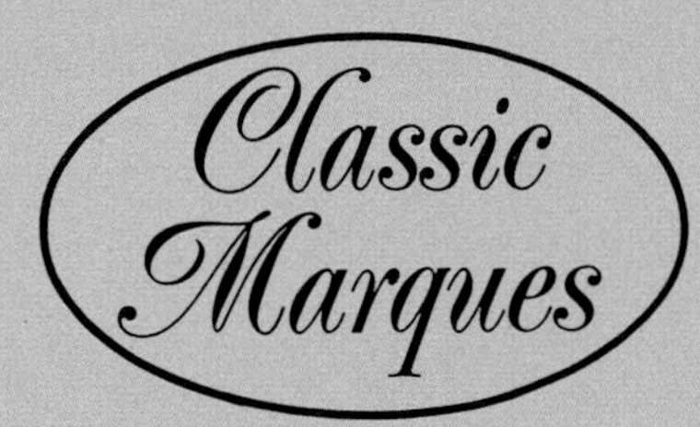

MUSTANG

Ian Penberthy

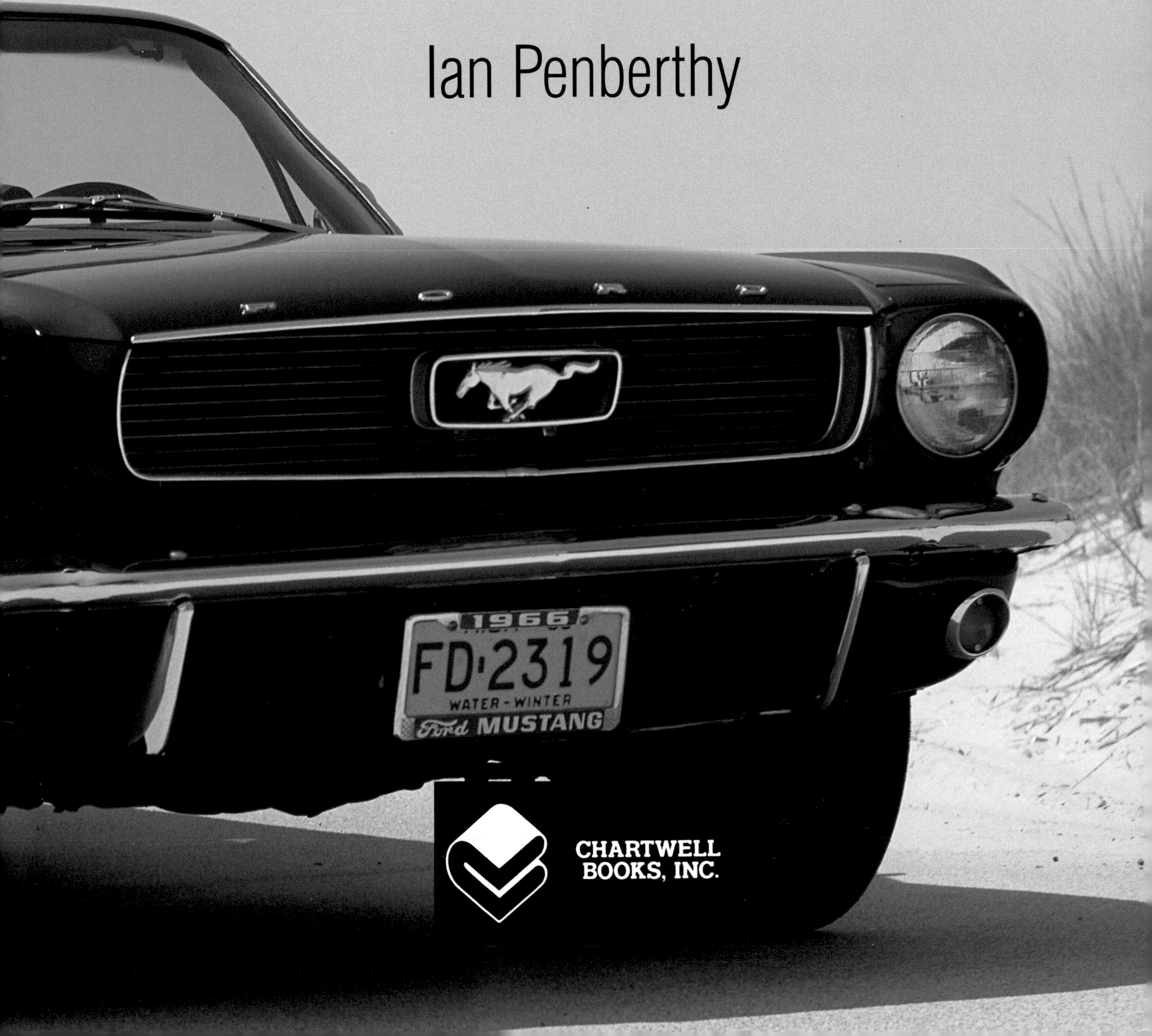

CHARTWELL BOOKS, INC.

First published in 1995 by
Book Sales, Inc.
114 Northfield Avenue
Raritan Center
Edison, N.J. 08818

Produced by
Brompton Books Corp.
15 Sherwood Place
Greenwich, CT 06830

ISBN 0-7858-0226-6

Printed in China

PAGE 1: Most sought after of the classic Mustangs today are the Shelby models, particularly the early cars that were actually converted by Carroll Shelby Motors. This 1967 Shelby GT500 Mustang was the first of the Shelbys to receive the 428cu.in. big-block V8.

PAGES 2-3: The '66 Mustang differed in little but detail to the 1965 model. Such was the runaway success of the original ponycar that there was no need to make major changes.

THESE PAGES: The popularity of the Mustang with young buyers led, inevitably, to them being hopped up even beyond the range of factory performance options offered. This '66 hardtop has received a set of CenterLine aluminum wheels and rear-mounted traction bars.

Contents

Introduction

There has always been a traditional rivalry between Ford Motor Company and the Chevrolet division of General Motors; both vie for the same market, thus any success that one has with a particular model is bound to affect the plans and decisions of the other. Over the years, the lead in styling and engineering innovation has passed back and forth between them, invariably to the benefit of the customer.

Back in the Fifties, Chevrolet were losing ground to Ford with a product line that was decidedly yesterday's news. Then, the advent of their 265cu.in. small-block V8 turned the tables. This light, powerful engine, teamed with a new range of sedans, gave Chevy a much-needed sportier image. Ford didn't have a comparable engine until the early Sixties when they introduced their lightweight 260cu.in. small-block V8.

The Fifties had also seen Chevrolet launch the two-seat Corvette sportscar, whereupon Ford's response was to bring out the two-seat Thunderbird. Altogether more 'civilized' than the Corvette, the T'bird sold in far greater numbers, but was only to remain in production in two-seat form for three years (until 1957). Despite the fact that the Thunderbird easily outsold the Corvette, it was not deemed

profitable enough for Ford. Consequently, for 1958, it grew into a full four-seater that would have a much wider market appeal and which sold in even greater numbers.

Thus, Chevrolet had the sporty-car market to themselves for a while. They weren't making any money out of it, but the Corvette was great at bringing people into Chevy dealers' showrooms – and they often left having bought another of the General's products. One such product was, like the Corvette, unusual for an American car. It was small, it was cheap to run and it had an aircooled, rear-mounted engine; it was the Corvair.

Chevrolet had launched the Corvair to fill what it saw as a need for a compact economy car; Ford had an answer – the Falcon, which was a conventional front-engined, rear-drive sedan, and it outsold the Corvair, just like the Thunderbird had wiped the floor with the Corvette. Then Chevrolet introduced the Corvair Monza, a much sportier version of the rear-engined compact and it was like they had opened the floodgates. They had stumbled on a niche in the market that hadn't been noticed before: there was a definite need for a car that offered sporting performance, handling and looks at a reasonable price without going to the extremes of the pure sports/racer as epitomized by the Corvette.

Sales of the Corvair Monza rocketed and Chevrolet responded with even more powerful models. Naturally, the rest of the industry scrambled to produce rivals in the sporty compact field: Ford's was the Falcon Futura, which appeared in 1961 and was followed by the Falcon Futura Sprint in 1963. The latter came with the new 260cu.in. small-block motor which gave the car a much-needed shot in the arm in terms of performance. Even so, the Corvair Monza was still streets ahead in numbers sold; the Falcon just didn't have the appeal of its rear-engined competitor.

To get the better of Chevrolet, Ford needed a new car, something that would offer sporting performance and sporting good looks, something that would appeal to the burgeoning 'youth' market. They already had a suitable powerplant in the lightweight V8; soon they would be entering a new thoroughbred in the race and it would gallop right into the lead.

BELOW: In 1968 Ford took over development of the Shelby cars and fitted the GT500 with the 428 Cobra Jet motor, whereupon it became the GT500KR (King of the Road).

OHIO
QTH-512
WILLIAMS

Chapter 1
A One-Horse Race

When Ford introduced their new sporting compact on 17 April 1964, it caused a sensation – dealers were swamped with people wanting to get a glimpse of the new car. The name on everybody's lips was 'Mustang.'

Available initially in two body styles with a list of options as long as your arm, the Mustang was just what Ford needed to take the lead from Chevrolet. It had crisp, sporting lines and, with the right options, performance to match; buyers could tailor the car to suit their own particular tastes, so it appealed to a wide spectrum of potential owners. And, although essentially it was very similar to the Falcon under the skin, even the automotive Press were generous with their praise. Ford had a winner on their hands, and a bigger winner than even they had imagined.

Although launched early in 1964 (April as opposed to the traditional September), the new Mustang was officially a 1965 model. From the outset, it had been designed as a four-seater, but back-seat room was a little limited. Buyers could choose between a two-door hardtop or convertible until September 1964, when those two body styles were joined by the sleek-looking Mustang 2+2 fastback. Whichever style was chosen, the Mustang was a racy, good-looking car with lots of appeal.

At the front, a shallow grille opening projected slightly ahead of the single headlights and contained a chrome sculpture of a running horse, which was to become the Mustang trademark for years to come. The sides of the car

ABOVE LEFT: When the Mustang was launched in April 1964, two models were available: a two-door hardtop and a convertible. The latter had a manually-operated top, which looked a lot better stowed than when it was up. Even so, the Mustang convertible was a good-looking car that had plenty of appeal.

LEFT: This 1966 convertible is equipped with the optional GT package that featured, among other things, twin driving lights set in the grille. The simulated rear brake scoop trim was also deleted when this option was specified.

ABOVE RIGHT: 1965 Mustangs had this running horse emblem on each front fender.

RIGHT: The 1965 hardtop was a clean design that offered the required degree of sportiness without the many drawbacks of a true sportscar.

were molded to form simulated scoop shapes ahead of the rear wheel wells, while the back panel carried neat clusters of triple tail lights and a central fuel filler cap. On the fastback 2+2, the rear roof pillars featured air extractor louvers which enhanced the sporty look of this particular model even further. In total, the car measured 181.6in. long (the same as the Falcon), 68.2in. wide and 51in. high.

The interior continued the sporty theme with individual front bucket seats and a small rear bench (the 2+2 had an optional fold-flat back seat to provide a large load platform); a front bench seat was optional, but didn't get many takers. There was a deep-dish steering wheel and a strip-type speedometer similar to that used in the Falcon.

Beneath the skin, the Mustang was very much based on Falcon components, including the chassis, although at 108in. the wheelbase was a little less than that of the former. Front suspension comprised wishbones, coil springs and telescopic shock absorbers, while at the rear a solid axle was suspended by parallel leaf springs and telescopic shock absorbers. Track was 56in. front and rear. Non-assisted, 9in. diameter, hydraulic drum brakes were standard on all four wheels, which were of 13in. diameter. All basic stuff.

In base form, the drivetrain was not too exciting, either. The standard engine was a 170cu.in. overhead-valve

LEFT: Destined to be a Mustang trademark for several years was the cluster of three rear lights.

BELOW LEFT: Much of the early Mustang was based on Ford's compact sedan, the Falcon, and this heritage was belied by the strip-type speedometer. This convertible has the Rally-Pac, which included steering-column-mounted tachometer and clock.

RIGHT: Some months after the initial launch of the car, Ford introduced a Mustang fastback coupe, and characteristic of this model were roof-pillar-mounted air vents.

BELOW: That Falcon-style speedometer. Note that this car has the optional air conditioning unit hung beneath the dashboard.

LEFT: Even with the top up, the '65 convertible was certainly a pretty car. One option was a luggage rack for the trunk lid.

RIGHT: When the Mustang was launched, it could be ordered with a 170cu.in. straight six engine or a small-block V8. The latter came in 260 and 289cu.in. versions. The 289 shown here developed 271bhp.

BELOW: Six months after the Mustang was introduced, the fastback Mustang 2+2 appeared. Its sloping roofline gave the car an even sportier look. This version has optional wire-wheel trims. The 2+2 had a separate trunk lid, unlike later models, and the option of a fold-down rear seat to increase luggage capacity.

straight six equipped with a single-barrel carburetor and with a rated output of 101bhp. Behind this was a three-speed manual gearbox complete with floor shifter, which was essential for the sporting image. Later in that first year, a 200cu.in. inline six, developing 120bhp, replaced the original engine.

This basic package was relatively inexpensive, but where the Mustang really scored was with its wide range of available extras that allowed the buyer to uprate the standard car to match his or her needs and pocket. The options covered every area of the car: powertrain, suspension, brakes, steering, wheels and tires, interior and so on.

Instead of the basic inline six, the Mustang could be ordered with a choice of more powerful engines: initially, 164bhp 260cu.in. and 210bhp 289cu.in. V8s (the latter was a development of the former). Later, a 271bhp 289 was added to the list, the 260 was dropped in favor of a 200bhp 289 and the 210bhp engine jumped to 225bhp.

There were optional transmissions, too: a three-speed manual with overdrive, a four-speed manual and Cruise-O-Matic three-speed automatic. The four-speed was mandatory with the high-power V8 as was a tougher rear axle with 3.89:1 or 4.11:1 gearing. A limited-slip differential was available. The V8s also came with 10in. diameter brake drums and 14in. wheels. These could be regular steel disk wheels with decorative covers or special sculpted versions.

There were packages to uprate the suspension to improve handling, the brakes (power assistance and later front disks), the steering (power assistance and quicker ratio) and

the interior (additional instruments, center console, special upholstery). Air conditioning was also offered for all cars except those equipped with the 271bhp V8 engine.

Although the standard car would not necessarily light any fires – the Press were disappointed with its performance – with the high-power V8, the Mustang could reach 60mph from rest in a little over 8 seconds. And when equipped with the optional handling package (stiffer springs and shock absorbers, front anti-roll bar, quicker steering and larger wheels and tires), it would really cling to the road.

Despite the fact that the base Mustang was very much a Falcon under the skin, its sporty styling and comprehensive options list hit the mark; dealers were besieged with orders and by the time the 1966 model was announced, in September 1965, Ford had sold some 680,989 '65 models – almost three times what they expected. The phenomenal success of the Mustang would rock the industry and set Ford's competitors scrambling to introduce their own versions of what would soon become known as the 'ponycar,' but for now Ford was several lengths ahead of the field.

When the 1966 Mustangs appeared, there was little to distinguish them visually from their predecessors. Indeed, there was little reason for Ford to make any changes: the Mustang had been a runaway success from the day it was launched and there was nothing comparable on offer from the opposition. There were changes, but they were mostly of a minor nature.

One area that was tidied up was the grille, which lost the horizontal chrome bars on each side of the central horse motif, so that the latter appeared to float in the center (the bars did return, however, on cars equipped with the GT options package and had auxiliary driving lights at their ends). All cars received 14in. diameter wheels with redesigned wheel covers, although the sixes still retained their 9in. drum brakes. The simulated scoop shapes in the car's sides also received a chrome trim ahead of the wheel well on all models except the 2+2 and those equipped with the GT pack.

Inside, one change that was immediately noticeable was the instrument panel. No longer dominated by the wide strip-type speedometer, this comprised a cluster of five

ABOVE LEFT: Few changes were made to the Mustang for 1966, but one obvious difference was the running horse emblem in the grille which now floated in the center.

ABOVE: Wire wheel trims were an option which gave the sporty Mustang an even sportier look.

RIGHT: Another external change was to the imitation brake scoop ahead of the rear wheels. This received a trim with three chrome strakes, although it wasn't fitted to the 2+2.

round gauges that previously had been available only as part of the GT options package. A large central speedometer was flanked by smaller gauges for fuel contents, water temperature, oil pressure and amps. These could be supplemented by a tachometer and clock that were mounted to the steering column and came as part of the Rally Pac option, which had been offered with the original '65 Mustang.

Mechanically, there was little difference between the '66 and the '65 Mustangs; the four engine options continued, but the Cruise-O-Matic transmission was offered with the high-power V8 for the first time. The V8-engined cars provoked far more interest than the sixes, but to celebrate the millionth Mustang built (early in 1966) and promote the six-cylinder car, Ford introduced the Sprint 200 option group. This was applicable to all three body styles with the 200cu.in. inline six only and included such features as wire wheel covers, an interior center console and special paintwork for the exterior.

As the 1966 model year came to a close, interest in the Mustang was still running high; the cars were selling as fast as they ever had, but the other runners in the race were beginning to make ground on the leader. A herd of ponies from other stables was galloping over the horizon. Fortunately, Ford had refreshed their own steed for 1967.

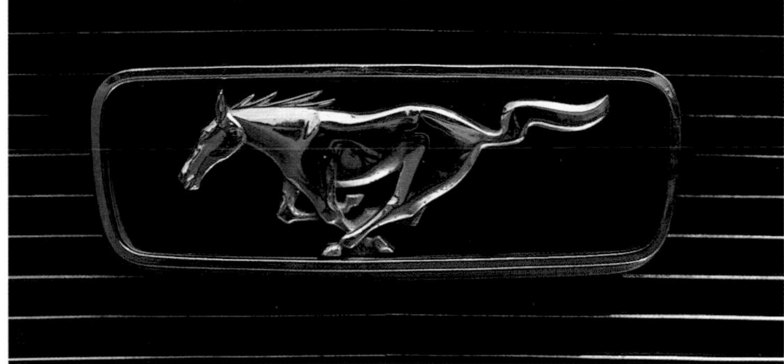

ABOVE: This clean '66 convertible sports a number of optional accessories, including the sculpted chrome wheels, the trunk-mounted luggage rack and rocker panel trims.

ABOVE RIGHT: All the classic Mustangs wore the running horse emblem.

LEFT: With the top up, the '66 Mustang still looks good.

RIGHT: All '66 Mustangs received this five-dial instrument panel, previously only available with the optional GT package.

Chapter 2
More Horsepower

For 1967 the Mustang took on a slightly more refined appearance, and Ford took the opportunity to improve the product even more. This was just as well, because 1967 saw the arrival of the Chevrolet Camaro and Pontiac Firebird from General Motors, two cars that were pitched right at the Mustang's market. Moreover, other ponycars were on the way from all the major manufacturers and even Ford themselves. So the Mustang no longer had a clear run, but brand loyalty and the fact that the Mustang had been the car that had started the whole ponycar race ensured that sales were still good.

At first glance, the Mustang looked the same, but on closer examination, it was clear that the body was quite a bit different to the earlier models. For a start, although built on what was essentially the same floorpan and chassis with the same wheelbase, it was 2in. longer and almost 3in. wider than before. The grille opening was deeper and pulled farther forward, giving the car a more purposeful look.

The sculptured sides with the imitation scoops ahead of the rear wheels were still in evidence and accentuated by two small grilles that appeared on all models. There was a more pronounced kick-up in the beltline immediately behind the doors, while the rear panel had been made concave. The latter still featured triple rear lights and a centrally-mounted fuel filler cap.

ABOVE LEFT: Although still recognizably a Mustang, the '67 model was longer, the grille having been enlarged and pulled forward. This gave the front end a more purposeful look. This convertible has been fitted with aftermarket wheels.

LEFT: The two-door hardtop remained a popular model in 1967. It still featured the triple tail light clusters, albeit of a slightly different design to match the concave rear panel. The GTA designation shows that the car was ordered with the GT package, but with an automatic transmission. All '67 models had a pair of imitation rear brake cooling scoops in their flanks.

One interesting feature of the '67 Mustang came as part of the Exterior Decor options group. This was a hood with two reversed air scoops let into the surface and containing turn-signal repeaters as a reminder to the driver.

All three body styles were still offered, the 2+2 having a delightful sweeping full fastback that ran unbroken right down to the very tail, unlike its predecessor which had a notch-back style. It retained the rear pillar vents, however, albeit in a slightly more restrained style.

There were changes beneath the skin too, changes that would bring benefits in both handling and performance. The front suspension was redesigned to put the coil springs above the upper wishbones (in common with other Fords of the period) and to widen the track by fractionally over 2in. The latter not only provided improvements in handling and ride, but it also allowed the engine compartment to be made wider. This was essential to accommodate a new engine option that year – the 390cu.in. big-block V8 that was used in some of Ford's larger sedans.

The 390 engine produced 320bhp, but by no stretch of the imagination could it be called a high-performance engine since its breathing was severely restricted and the design precluded running it at high rpm. However, by virtue of its long stroke, it developed lots of torque at relatively low engine speed and, when backed by the four-speed manual gearbox and a suitable rear axle ratio, it could propel the Mustang to mid 7 second 0-60mph times. Moreover, it was quite a bit cheaper than the high-power, high-revving small block 289.

Unfortunately, the big-block 390 was very much heavier than the smaller engine and promoted serious understeer. This could be alleviated to a degree by specifying the Competition Handling Package with, among other items, stiffer springs, adjustable shock absorbers, anti-roll bar and 15in. wheels. This equipment, however, could only be obtained if ordered with the GT options group. Among other things, this included power-assisted front disk brakes, dual exhausts and foglamps mounted in the grille opening.

The availability of the big-block engine in the Mustang came at the right time, for the competition from GM also had big-block V8 options – the Camaro with Chevy's 396 and the Firebird with a 400cu.in. motor. Both generated more power than Ford's 390, as much as 375bhp in the Chevy's case. It was the beginning of a cubic inch war, the ponycars receiving bigger and bigger engines as the years rolled by.

In addition to the 390, the '67 Mustang could also be ordered with any of the three 289cu.in. engines from 1966

LEFT: Few changes were made for 1968, as this convertible shows. The simulated brake cooling scoops were deleted, however.

RIGHT: A special model of Mustang that was built in 1968 was the GT/CS California Special. Based on the two-door hardtop, it came with a Shelby trunk lid and side scoops, sequential tail lights and special striping.

BELOW: '68 models had a redesigned instrument panel and steering wheel.

BELOW RIGHT: On '67 and '68 Mustangs, the grille was pulled forward, leading to deeper headlight buckets.

BOTTOM RIGHT: Sequential tail lights used on the GT/CS were similar to those used on the Shelby cars.

which retained the same bhp ratings as before – 200, 225 and 271. As then, the base engine was the 200cu.in. inline six. Also the same were the transmission options: all engines, with the exception of the high-power 289, were offered with a three-speed manual gearbox as standard. The 271bhp 289 got the four-speed, which was optional on all the other V8s, while the six had the option of the three-speed automatic. The latter could also be had with any of the other engines.

The interior of the new Mustang received a revised instrument panel, this time dominated by two large-diameter gauges with three smaller dials above them. Interior options included a tilt-away steering wheel and air conditioning that could be built into the dashboard rather than hung beneath it like an afterthought as before.

So with the '67 Mustang, Ford still had a frontrunner, but the competition was moving up and beginning to take sales away from the original ponycar. This would continue for 1968 when there would be few visual differences to set the later car apart from its predecessor. However, there would be some interesting developments under the skin that would push the performance envelope even further.

Externally, there were minor modifications to the grille that saw the horse motif set flush with its surface, while the chrome bars that came with the foglamps in the GT options pack were also dropped. Side marker lamps at front and rear were new, as was an optional contrasting color stripe to outline the body side creasing – again part of the GT options.

The big news that year was the engine range, which saw several changes. As before, the base engine was the 200 cu.in. inline six, now rated at 115bhp in the light of changes necessary to meet government exhaust emission standards. Next came the only 289 small-block V8 offered

that year, which developed 195bhp, followed by a stroked version of this engine with a capacity of 302cu.in. and a power rating of 230bhp. The 390cu.in. big-block now produced 325bhp and was joined by an even bigger engine, the race-bred 427 which pumped out 390bhp. Unlike the 390, this engine was built with performance in mind and had a much stronger bottom end, more efficient lubrication system and better breathing. Strangely, this engine option, which was very expensive, was only available with the automatic transmission. Even so, 0-60mph times approaching 6 seconds were possible with this combination. Another mandatory option with this and the 390 V8 were power-assisted front disk brakes.

Despite the incredible performance imparted to the

Mustang by the 427, it did not get a lot of takers, probably because of the cost and because it made the Mustang a difficult car to handle. Consequently, it was dropped from the options list before the end of the model year. In its place came the 428 Cobra Jet. Rated at 335bhp, this big-block V8 used heads that were similar to the 427's but with larger intake ports, together with the same camshaft. However, its bore and stroke were different, leading to greater torque at lower engine rpm. Part of the package was a Ram Air induction system whereby functional hood scoops were connected directly to the carburetor by means of a special flap valve. The engine could be backed by a four-speed manual gearbox or Ford C6 three-speed automatic.

Cars equipped with the Cobra Jet engine option came with other changes too; in fact, it was a definite model type. It featured stronger suspension, the rear shock absorbers being placed one in front of the axle and one behind to counteract axle tramp under hard acceleration. A stronger rear axle was also included.

Another special model introduced that year was the GT/CS, or California Special. Based on a hardtop with any of the available engine options, the GT/CS was distinguished by a number of trim options that made it stand out from the rest of the Mustang crowd. Among these were a blacked-out grille, foglamps and non-functioning side scoops, spoilered trunk lid and sequential tail lights like those used on the Shelby Mustang (see Chapter 5). Distinctive side stripes completed the package.

Similar special Mustangs were produced for other areas too, indicating that Ford were no longer having it all their own way in the sales race. Even so, Mustang was still undisputed leader in the ponycar race, but the herd was catching up: Ford would have to run faster still.

MARIE'S 69
MUSTANG

Chapter 3
Flexing Some Muscle

Ford's Mustang underwent another restyling exercise for 1969 and grew a little more in the process. The body, that was still unmistakably a Mustang, was an inch wider and nearly 4in. longer, although the wheelbase remained the same at 108in. The car was also 1.5in. lower than the previous model. As a result, the Mustang looked even more powerful than before – with the right options, it was too.

For 1969, the grille opening had been enlarged still further and pulled forward to stretch the nose of the car. Headlights flanked the grille as before, but a second pair was installed in the grille opening in place of the previously fitted optional foglamps. The hood received a tapering power bulge that ran down the center, while the windshield was laid back a little to accentuate the sweeping lines of the body. The sides were cleaned up by the removal of the previous sculpturing and imitation rear brake scoops, while the rear lights changed to flat-lens units rather than the usual concave type of before.

The same three body styles were available, but the fastback was given a lower roofline in keeping with the raked windshield, which gave it an even more purposeful look. This was emphasized all the more by scoops in the tops of the rear fenders, immediately behind the door handles, and by a spoiler lip formed in the rear panel. To match this more aggressive look, the fastback body style was referred to as the SportsRoof.

A benefit of the larger body was a roomier interior, and rear-seat passengers were given more legroom. The interior was restyled, too, and had a new instrument panel with two large gauges and a smaller gauge to each side. Various interior options were available including such features as a center console, high-back bucket seats and woodgrain trim panels.

The running gear and suspension remained pretty much the same as in the '68 model, but there were changes to the engine options. As before, the base engine was the 200cu.in. six, but a 250cu.in. inline six was also available and was good for 155bhp. Next came a 220bhp 302 small-block V8, and the option list also included the 390cu.in. big-block. The 428 Cobra Jet engine was also there in three different versions. Two of these had a unique Ram Air induction system that incorporated a functional scoop which

LEFT: For 1969 the Mustang grew even more, the grille getting bigger and being pulled even farther forward. It was still flanked by a pair of headlights, but a second pair was actually mounted inside the grille opening as well. The convertible continued in production as well as the hardtop and 2+2, although the last was renamed the SportsRoof.

RIGHT: The convertible looked even better with the roof down. All three models lost the side sculpturing that had been a Mustang trademark since the launch, although the soft and hardtops still had a form of simulated scoop ahead of the rear wheels.

LEFT: To go with the new exterior, Mustangs for 1969 also had a new interior including a redesigned instrument panel and steering wheel.

RIGHT: The 1969 Mach 1 had race-track styling to go with a high level of performance. Based on the SportsRoof body style, the Mach 1 came with the 250bhp 351W engine, uprated suspension and a deluxe interior. Exterior features included a blacked-out hood with air scoop and optional NASCAR-type hold-down pins.

BELOW: The Mach 1 was distinctively marked.

BELOW RIGHT: Compared to the original Mustang of 1965, the '69 model had grown quite a lot.

was mounted directly to the carburetor. The scoop protruded through a hole in the hood and consequently could be seen to move as the engine rocked on its mounts; it was christened the Shaker scoop for obvious reasons. This induction system was also available on other large V8s in the Mustang range.

A new engine had also been added to the range, a revised long-stroke motor based on the 302 which boasted 351cu.in. and came in 250 and 290bhp versions. This new engine was one of two 351cu.in. V8s in Ford's inventory and there were considerable differences between the two. In 1969, the Mustang was equipped with the 351 Windsor engine (351W), so called because it was built at Ford's Canadian engine plant in Windsor, Ontario; the other 351 was built in Cleveland, Ohio, and identified in the same way (351C). The 351C engine would make its debut in the Mustang in 1970.

A three-speed manual gearbox was the standard offering with all engines with the exception of the 290 and 428. A four-speed was optional, as was the automatic on all the engines.

Keen to hold on to as much of the ponycar market as possible in the face of increased competition from their rivals, Ford added some special models of the Mustang to its line-up for 1969. One of these was a luxury version known as the Grande and based on the hardtop. It came with extra soundproofing and the deluxe interior options as standard. The exterior was brightened up with wire wheel covers, chrome trims to the wheel wells and rocker panels, a two-tone stripe along the sides and color co-ordinated door mirrors.

By contrast, the Mach 1 Mustang emphasized the high-performance aspect of the car with styling and mechanical features that smacked of the race track. As standard, the Mach 1 was offered with the 250bhp version of the 351W engine, but it could be ordered with any of the standard Mustang V8 options. The car also came with uprated suspension but, surprisingly, drum brakes all round, although wise buyers specified the optional front disk brakes as well.

LEFT: This Shaker hood scoop was optional on engines equipped with Ram Air induction. It was mounted to the top of the carburetor and, consequently, moved with the engine, hence the name.

BELOW: The limited-production Boss 302 was a really hot performer capable of generating more power than its official 290bhp rating. Again based on the SportsRoof, it came with front and rear spoilers and distinctive paintwork.

BELOW RIGHT: The SportsRoof styling was ideal for the performance Mustangs such as the Mach 1; it was sleek with a low roof line. Note the scoops in the rear quarters.

Inside, the Mach 1 came with the same deluxe interior as the Grande, including the soundproofing package, but it was the exterior that really promoted the performance image. Based on the sleek SportsRoof body style only, the Mach 1 came with a matt black hood that featured an aggressive-looking scoop (or it could have the Shaker scoop of the Ram Air set-up). The hood could also be equipped with NASCAR-type quick-release hold-down pins to stress the race-car look even further. Bold side stripes and special chromed steel wheels set off the package.

The Mach 1 wasn't the end of the story as far as high-performance 1969 Mustangs were concerned, however, as Ford had something even more exciting to offer on a limited basis. This was the Boss 302, a car that was built to allow Ford to introduce a high-performance version of the 302cu.in. engine for use in the Sports Car Club of America's Trans-Am series of races. According to the rules, Ford had to sell 1000 copies of the engine to the public before it was eligible to race, hence the Boss 302 Mustang.

Officially rated at 290bhp, but clearly capable of generating more power, the Boss 302 engine came with a stronger cylinder block and bottom end, big-valve heads, solid valve lifters and a 780cfm Holley four-barrel carburetor on an aluminum high-rise inlet manifold. It was backed by a four-speed manual gearbox and would push the Mustang to sub 7 second 0-60mph times.

There was more to the Boss 302 than the engine, though. As with the Mach 1, it was based on the SportsRoof body but without the non-functional side scoops of the standard car. Matt black was used on the hood, around the headlights and on the rear panel, while a distinctive C-stripe adorned each side. At the front, there was a large spoiler to prevent the nose from rising at speed, while this could be offset by an optional adjustable wing-type spoiler for mounting to the rear deck. A set of rear window slats was also available, while wide sculptured steel wheels completed an impressive-looking package.

Beneath the skin, suspension, braking and steering im-

provements meant that the Boss 302 was much more than just a straight-line sprinter. It handled as well as it went and provided Ford with a successful racing package.

There was yet another race-inspired Mustang for 1969 – the Boss 429. Once again, it was developed to allow Ford to introduce a new, powerful competition engine, this time for NASCAR (National Association for Stock Car Automobile Racing) events. The rules said that Ford had to sell 500 such engines to the public, and while in competition they would be used in Torinos, the company chose to make them available in the Mustang.

The Boss 429 was based on an existing Ford design, but it had a beefier cast-iron cylinder block. It featured a strong bottom end with four-bolt main caps, forged crankshaft and rods and aluminum heads with big valves and part-hemispherical combustion chambers. Although equipped with hydraulic valve lifters, a mild camshaft and a small four-barrel carburetor that restricted breathing somewhat, the Boss 429 pumped out 375bhp. Behind the engine was a close-ratio four-speed manual gearbox which passed the power to either a Detroit Locker or Traction Lok rear axle with 4.30:1 or 3.91:1 gearing respectively.

Installing the big 429 engine required considerable changes around the front end of the car, since the existing engine bay was not wide enough. To make enough room, it was necessary to place the battery in the trunk and move the suspension mountings outboard, thus increasing the front track, which provided a bonus in improved handling. The suspension mountings were also strengthened at the same time and the suspension itself uprated with stronger springs and anti-roll bars at front and rear. There were improvements to the braking system by means of power-assisted front disks and to the steering, which was also power-assisted. The result was a Mustang that could not only out-run its stablemates, but also out-handle practically all of them, too.

The Boss 429 was based on the standard SportsRoof with the addition of a large hood scoop and front spoiler. It was much more subdued in appearance when compared with the Boss 302, having no striping or matt black paintwork,

ABOVE: The Mustang was given a few styling changes for 1970 and most powerful in the line-up was the Boss 429 which pumped out 375bhp. Fewer than 500 of these cars were built for 1970.

ABOVE RIGHT: Given its performance potential, the Boss 429 was very understated in appearance, but the spoilers give the game away.

RIGHT: The monster Boss 429 engine was developed for NASCAR racing where it was fitted to the Torino; the Mustang was the only road-going Ford to have the engine.

although it did have the same sculpted steel wheels. It also came with a deluxe interior.

As 1970 rolled around, the Mustang range continued pretty much as it was, but with a few changes here and there. Most noticeable was that the outer pair of headlights had been deleted and replaced by a pair of air inlets, while the non-functioning rear fender scoops had also been dropped. At the rear, the tail lights were now recessed into a flat panel. Inside, high-back bucket seats came as standard and there was a new style of three-spoke steering wheel.

The engine options continued as before with the exception of the 390cu.in. big-block and the 290bhp 351W, both of which were no longer available. There were two new engines, however, both versions of Ford's other 351 – the Cleveland engine. A two-barrel carbureted 351C developed 250bhp, while the other was equipped with a four-barrel carburetor and gave 300bhp.

Although based on the same bore and stroke dimensions as the 351W, the Cleveland engine had far superior breathing characteristics, featuring heads with bigger ports and valves. There were two different sets of heads to match the two- and four-barrel carburetors.

There were changes to the appearance of the performance Mustangs in addition to the body changes. The Mach 1, for instance, received full-length aluminum rocker panel covers containing 'Mach 1' lettering in place of the previous side stripes, and the black paint on the hood was restricted to a central stripe the width of the air scoop.

The Boss 302 had an even more dramatic stripe that ran up the center of the hood, split and ran across over the fender tops and down to run back along the sides of the car. The Boss 429 received a black-painted hood scoop in place of the previously color-keyed example.

For 1969, Ford had sold just a little short of 300,000 Mustangs, but by the end of the 1970 model year that had dropped to 190,727. The competition was breathing hard on the original ponycar's neck, while the market as a whole was shrinking. The next move could be critical to the Mustang's future; unfortunately, it would be the wrong move for the car's image.

LEFT: For 1970, the front end was changed once more: a pair of headlights still resided in the grille opening, but the pair that flanked the grille was dropped in favor of gill-like air vents. The rest of the bodywork remained essentially the same. The hardtop continued in production, as did the convertible and SportsRoof.

ABOVE: Regional specials were still being built in 1970, among them the Twister Special. Sold purely in the Kansas City area, the Twister Special was based on a Mach 1, came in Grabber Orange only and had distinctive markings.

RIGHT: Only 96 Twister Specials were built, half of them having the 428 Super Cobra Jet engine with Ram Air and the Shaker hood scoop like this one.

Chapter 4
From Muscle to Flab

Throughout the years from its introduction in 1964, with each successive restyle, the Mustang had got bigger. That was to happen again for the 1971 cars. Now based on a 109in. wheelbase, the Mustang had grown in width by nearly 2.5in. and in length by just over 2in. Moreover, it was heavier than in 1970 – over 200lb heavier. The lithe, taut, compact package that had been the first Mustang – and which had led to much of its appeal – was no more. The result was a heavy-looking car that was a long way from the original concept. For the time being, however, the Mustang still offered rip-snorting performance, although it was being steadily emasculated by the need to meet increasingly stringent exhaust emission standards.

The 1971 restyle was probably the most radical change from one year to another, and without the familiar emblems, it might not have been immediately obvious that this car was a Mustang. At the front, a full-width grille opening contained the outline of the old Mustang grille and a pair of headlights, while a large expanse of hood ran back to an even more steeply raked windshield than before. The back edge of the hood was kicked up to conceal the windshield wipers.

Like the '70 models, the latest Mustang had no scoops in the sides – in fact, they were very smooth – and there was a very pronounced kick-up on the rear quarters immediately behind the doors. A flat rear panel contained new light units that were still divided into three sections but bore no resemblance to anything used before.

All three body styles continued in production, but the hardtop had 'flying buttress' rear roof pillars that swept down in a continuous curve to the tail. Far more radical was the SportsRoof, the rear window of which was mounted at a very shallow angle indeed. This was not only difficult for the driver to see out of, but with the associated shallow angle of the roof as it flowed to the tail, it gave the rear end of the car a very heavy look.

Along with the new body came a new interior, but still with high-back bucket seats. The instrument panel contained two large gauges for the speedometer and all functions other than the fuel gauge, which was a separate, smaller gauge between the two large ones. An optional tachometer was available to fill one of the large gauge positions, in which case, the oil pressure, water temperature and amps gauges were mounted above the radio in the center of the dashboard. Most of the regular interior options were available: center console, air conditioning, tilt steering wheel, wood trim panels and so on.

As usual, the base engine was an inline six, but this time it was the 250cu.in. engine that had been an option in the previous year. Smallest of the V8s was a 210bhp 302, while the 351W engine had been dropped. At first two 351C engines were included in the engine options list, one with a

ABOVE LEFT: The last restyle of the classic Mustang occurred in 1971, and it was a move in the wrong direction, the car becoming even larger and heavier. However, the Mach 1 was still available to provide a performance image.

LEFT: An optional instrument package provided an 8000rpm tachometer in the left-hand pod and a cluster of three gauges in the center of the dash panel.

RIGHT: The Mach 1 came with a range of engines including the 285bhp 351 V8.

LEFT: Performance Mustangs for 1971 could be specified with the NASA hood, which incorporated a good number of scoops. If these were functional, the hood carried the 'Ram Air' label.

RIGHT: The Boss 351 was the last of the Boss Mustangs to be built and offered an integrated package of high performance with looks to match.

BELOW: The Mach 1 continued to carry distinctive badging.

two-barrel carburetor developing 240bhp and the other with a four-barrel that put out 285bhp. These were joined later in the year by a Cobra Jet version of the engine that developed 280bhp.

One reason for the larger bodyshell had been to accommodate the largest of the Mustang engine options that year: a 429cu.in. big-block. This was not the race-inspired motor from the Boss 429, but rather an engine based on the standard components that had appeared in the larger Ford sedans of the day. The engine was given the Cobra Jet designation and came in three forms, much as the 428 had done before.

The basic 429 Cobra Jet engine, rated at 370bhp, had big-valve heads, a strengthened bottom end, hydraulic valve lifters and a Rochester Quadrajet four-barrel carburetor rated at 700cfm. It could be specified with or without Ram Air, but no longer was the Shaker scoop used. Instead, the hood incorporated two functional NASA ducts that were connected directly to the carburetor's air cleaner. The 429CJ engine could push the Mustang from rest to 60mph in around 6.5 seconds.

A 375bhp 429 was also offered. This engine had solid lifters, forged pistons and a Holley 780cfm four-barrel carburetor. With this engine, an optional Drag Pack became mandatory, giving the car a Detroit Locker or Traction Lok rear end with an appropriately low gear ratio. Also mandatory were power-assisted brakes and steering.

The inline six, 302 and two-barrel 351C came as standard with a three-speed manual gearbox, while the more powerful engines had a four-speed. An automatic was optional with all engines.

The rest of the running gear remained pretty much as it was in the previous year and could be uprated to improve handling by ordering the Competition Suspension package. This included variable-ratio power steering that provided much more 'feel' than before.

Once more, the Grande and Mach 1 luxury and performance versions of the Mustang were offered. The latter came

with a front spoiler, identifying side stripes and a matt black panel in the center of the hood, which incorporated the NASA ducts of the Ram Air installation. However, unless a Ram Air engine was specified, these were non-functional. The Mach 1 grille contained a pair of foglamps and the adjustable rear wing spoiler remained an option.

As standard, Mach 1s were offered with the 302 V8, but any of the bigger engines could be specified. Uprated suspension was standard fare, while 15in. sculptured steel wheels were optional.

In place of the Boss 302 there was the Boss 351, which continued the theme of the earlier race-inspired Mustang, offering similar levels of performance and handling. In appearance, the Boss 351 looked similar to the Mach 1, having the same sort of striping package, front spoiler and optional rear wing and wheels. The lower portions of the

RAM AIR
BOSS 351
MUSTANG
BFGoodrich
Radial T/A
71BOSS

LEFT: A unique model for 1972 was the Mustang Sprint which was available in either hardtop or SportsRoof form. Despite the name, it was not a performance-oriented version of the Mustang, but rather a cosmetic package.

RIGHT: All Mustang Sprints were finished in white with blue and red striping, and they carried a 'Stars and Stripes' decal on each rear fender. A special interior package co-ordinated with the exterior finish.

BELOW: Color-keyed rear-view mirrors were an integral part of the Sprint package.

BELOW RIGHT: Mustang styling changed hardly at all between the 1971 and 1972 models, but for 1973 there were changes, particularly to the front of the car. A new grille arrangement was installed with vertical parking lights inboard of the headlights. This would be the last year for Mustang convertibles for some time, and this example is kitted out with the optional 'slot mag' wheels, Ram Air and the exterior Decor Group package.

body and the hood were painted either black or silver to contrast with the main color, while the functional NASA-ducted hood was standard equipment.

Beneath the hood was an uprated version of the four-barrel 351C with solid lifters, a toughened crankshaft and forged conrods. With a compression ratio of 11:1 and a 750cfm Motorcraft four-barrel carburetor, the Boss 351 was officially rated at 330bhp, but this was a bit of an understatement given its ability to push the car to 60mph in under 6 seconds. Behind the engine was a four-speed manual gearbox. The Competition Suspension and big tires ensured good handling to match the acceleration.

Sadly the Boss 351 was not to be available for 1972 when the changes to the Mustang range were very limited. There was little to distinguish the '72 models from their immediate predecessors, but there was less emphasis on performance with many of the bigger engines being dropped. This left the 250cu.in. six, the 302cu.in. V8, the two-barrel 351C (with or without Ram Air) and the 351 Cobra Jet. These had respective bhp ratings of 98, 140, 177 and 266; part of the reason for the lower ratings was that Ford now quoted net bhp rather than gross. For a while, a High Output (HO) version of the 351C engine was made available. Based on the Boss 351 engine, it was rated at 275bhp and came with a

GOODYEAR 
EAGLE ST
Mustang
73
Mustang

package that included a four-speed gearbox, power-assisted front disk brakes, uprated suspension and a Traction Lok rear end.

One new model introduced that year was the Sprint which, essentially, was a cosmetic package applied to the hardtop and SportsRoof. All Sprints were painted white and came with red and blue stripes on the hood and along the lower body sides. A patriotic touch was a 'Stars and Stripes' shield added to each rear quarter.

For 1973, the engine options remained much as before, as did the three body styles. A new grille contained vertical parking lights, while all cars were fitted with a body-color front bumper designed to meet the government's 5mph collision standards. The rear bumper remained a chromed item. One change to the option list was that the 15in. sculptured steel wheels were replaced by 14in. forged aluminum slot wheels. Most other options remained the same.

Few other changes appeared for 1973, which would be the last year for the traditional ponycar: it had simply outgrown its market. Potential customers were switching to smaller cars or even imports which were now truer to the original Mustang concept than was the Mustang itself. In 1974 Ford would try to recapture the market with a new Mustang, but it would be a shadow of its former self; it would be the Eighties before another Mustang appeared to offer real ponycar appeal. For the moment, however, the Mustang would be able to manage little more than a trot.

ABOVE: 1973 would see the last of the first-generation Mustangs, which had outgrown their market. The SportsRoof appeared muscle-bound; it was heavier than ever and no longer offered the power it once had.

RIGHT: By 1973 the Mustang had lost much of its initial sporting appeal, having become very much just another mid-size, run-of-the-mill automobile.

OVERLEAF: Last of a breed. As 1973 came to a close, the original ponycar faced a bleak future. Could Ford recapture the market with a new breed?

Mustang

G.T. 350
65 SHELBY

SKIP & DAWN
CALIFORNIA
65 SHELBY
65 SHELBY

Chapter 5
From Carroll's Corral

Keen to stress the performance aspect of their new Mustang, Ford approached Carroll Shelby to develop a racing version that would dominate the race tracks and take the laurels away from their rivals, Chevrolet, who were enjoying considerable success in road racing events with the Corvette. They had good reason to turn to Shelby, for he was responsible for the highly successful Cobra sportscar, a marriage of the diminutive English AC Ace and Ford's small-block V8.

Sold through a select number of Ford dealers, the Shelby Cobra had cleaned up in just about every event it entered, so Carroll Shelby was seen as the ideal person to give the Mustang a high-profile winning image. He did just that, too, as Shelby Mustangs won their class in the SCCA road racing championships three years in a row – 1965-67. To complement the racing versions of the car were production replicas available to the public.

The Shelby versions of the Mustang began to appear in 1965 and were based on the 2+2 body style only. They were completed at Shelby's Los Angeles facility before being made available through Ford's dealer network. Cars were delivered to Shelby minus the hood, rear seat and exhaust system and equipped with the 271bhp 289 small-block V8 and a four-speed manual gearbox.

Shelby then reworked the engine with an aluminum inlet manifold, larger Holley carburetor, tubular exhaust headers and a less-restrictive exhaust system that terminated just ahead of the rear wheels. These modifications allowed the engine to crank out 306bhp.

To match the improved performance, modifications were also made to the suspension, steering and braking systems. These included revised front-end geometry, stiffer springs, Koni adjustable shock absorbers, a hefty front anti-roll bar, rear traction bars, front disk brakes and larger rear drums, and revised Pitman and idler arms. Moreover, the front end was strengthened by the addition of bracing bars between the firewall and front shock absorber towers and between the towers themselves. At the rear, the axle was equipped with a Detroit Locker differential, while the battery was moved from the engine compartment to the trunk to improve weight distribution and assist traction.

Changes were also made to the exterior to make this Mustang stand out from the herd. In place of the standard steel hood was a fiberglass replica that incorporated a functional air scoop. The grille lost its central running horse emblem; instead the more subdued standard front fender emblem, complete with red, white and blue stripes, was used, being offset to one side. Two wide blue stripes ran down the center of the car, while each side carried additional striping and the legend 'GT350.' As standard, the Shelby came with 6 × 15in. steel wheels, although five-spoke Cragar wheels were optional.

ABOVE LEFT: When Ford launched the Mustang in 1965 they set out to underline the performance aspect of the car by making it a winner on the track. They turned to Carroll Shelby who took the pony and produced a charger. The white paint with optional blue stripes, fiberglass hood and large, functional scoop and Cragar wheels set the car apart – it performed to match.

LEFT: The '65 Shelby Mustang had a new front panel with an extra air inlet and a mesh grille that carried the Mustang emblem from the front fender of the standard car. Amazingly, Ford allowed Shelby to remove all the Ford badging from the car.

RIGHT: Shelby designated the car GT350, although this doesn't seem to have any particular significance in terms of horsepower or engine size.

Inside, changes were in keeping with the competition nature of the car. There was a dash-mounted pod that contained a tachometer and oil pressure gauge, the standard steering wheel was replaced by a woodrim item and both front seats had genuine competition seat belts. Curiously, the standard Mustang strip-type speedometer was retained, given that the optional GT five-gauge unit would have been more in keeping with the theme of the car. In place of the rear seat was a fiberglass shelf which carried the spare wheel under a protective cover.

In this street trim, the Shelby GT350 could run from rest to 60mph in around 6.5 seconds; cars intended purely for competition were even quicker. The latter received a 330bhp version of the 289, a much larger fuel tank, a fiberglass front apron with massive air duct, plastic windows, racing seats, extra instruments and wider wheels.

The '65 Shelby Mustang was an exciting car to drive, but there was no denying that it was really a racer with just enough alterations to make it usable on the street. This was reflected in relatively limited sales – a total of 562 for the Mustang's first year of production.

Consequently, for 1966, the Shelby was made a little more civilized, although its excellent performance and handling did not suffer as a result. Externally, the car looked similar, but there was now a functional brake cooling scoop on each side ahead of the rear wheels, while the air extractor vents in the rear roof pillars were replaced with clear plastic windows. The car could be ordered in colors other than white, too, with or without the broad central stripes.

As for 1965, the engine in the Shelby was the 306bhp 289 small-block. However, this was available with an optional Paxton centrifugal supercharger that allowed the engine to develop over 400bhp – a real drag racer.

The civilizing process began with softer springs, standard shock absorbers and a conventional exhaust; the Koni shock absorbers and Detroit Locker differential became options. Another option was a Ford C4 automatic transmission. The wheels went down to 14in. diameter, being either sculptured five-spoke steel versions or special ten-spoke Shelby alloy items.

Inside, the '66 Shelby was equipped with a rear seat and the five-gauge instrument panel that had been an option in 1965, but now was standard on all Mustangs.

Shelby also built a number of GT350H models that year for, of all people, the Hertz car rental company. These had a unique black-and-gold paint scheme and chrome wheels and formed a part of the company's rental fleet. It was a good publicity exercise, which Hertz continued through 1967 and 1968, although after the first year the cars no longer carried the 'H' suffix. One thing for sure is that those 'rent-a-racers' must have led a very hard life indeed compared to other rental cars.

LEFT: For 1966, Shelby made the car a little more civilized and, as a result, Ford sold a lot more. The car was only available as a 2+2, and for '66 the rear roof pillar gills were replaced by clear plastic windows, while functional rear brake cooling scoops were added to the sides.

RIGHT: In the Shelby the small-block 289 produced 306bhp and came with special Cobra finned aluminum valve covers.

BELOW: In 1966, the Shelby Mustang could be ordered with these optional Shelby wheels.

BELOW RIGHT: The '66 Shelby had a functional brake cooling scoop set in the side of the bodywork ahead of the rear wheel.

There is no doubt that the civilizing process of the Shelby Mustang for 1966 helped boost sales of the special model, and this process would continue. As a result, sales would increase and the car would generate profits, but as with the standard Mustang, the Shelby would move inexorably away from the original concept.

With the advent of the restyled '67 Mustang, the Shelby also took on a new look, the liberal use of body scoops giving it a particularly aggressive appearance. Still based on the 2+2 fastback, the '67 Shelby was fitted with a fiberglass nosepiece incorporating an extra air duct below the grille, which contained an extra pair of headlights. As standard, these were mounted in the center of the opening, although some states required that they be moved outboard.

A fiberglass hood featured a large scoop, while additional scoops were attached to the rear roof pillars in place of the standard extractor vents. The rear brake cooling scoops were still in evidence. At the rear, a spoiler lip was incorporated in the deck, while the standard Mustang tail lights were replaced with long rectangular units available from Ford's Cougar.

The wheels had reverted to 15in. diameter and the customer could choose between standard steel wheels with hubcaps or two types of aluminum wheel. Underneath, the suspension was standard Mustang uprated with heavy-duty springs and shock absorbers; disk brakes were fitted to the front and drums to the rear. Inside, the car received additional instruments to cover oil pressure and amps, while a roll bar was installed together with inertia-reel seat belts.

The same engine/transmission package was offered for the GT350, but 1967 also saw the introduction of the GT500 which came with the big-block 428cu.in. V8. This had dual four-barrel carburetors on an aluminum manifold and pushed out 355bhp. A few GT500s came with Ford's 427cu.in. V8, a race-bred motor with forged crank, rods and aluminum pistons, solid lifters and dual four-barrels.

Despite the engine options in the Shelby Mustangs, which still produced plenty of performance, they were no longer race cars let loose on the street. They were much easier to drive and much more comfortable than the original, and this was borne out by increased sales – 3225 Shelbys for 1967.

For 1968, Ford was intent on making the Shelby pay its way and had taken over the development of the car completely. It featured a restyled front end with large grille openings above and below the front bumper, while the fiberglass hood was given louvers on each side. The grille-mounted headlights were dropped and Thunderbird sequential tail lights replaced the Cougar items at the rear.

ABOVE, FAR LEFT: Shelby manufactured wheels too, including these impressive wires.

ABOVE LEFT: By 1967 the Shelby Mustang was beginning to look quite aggressive. These rear roof pillar scoops and brake cooling scoops reinforce that look.

ABOVE: Shelby dropped Ford's big 428 motor into the Mustang in 1967 to produce the GT500. It filled the engine compartment. Note the braces between the shock towers and firewall.

RIGHT: Just like the GT350, the GT500 came with rocker panel stripes identifying it as such.

OVERLEAF: Both GT350 and GT500 had a new fiberglass front end incorporating a wide hood scoop. A unique feature was the pair of headlights in the center of the grille.

G.T.500

LEFT: The front end treatment was revised again for 1968, by which time Ford had taken over the project completely from Shelby, although the car still retained the latter's name.

RIGHT: 1968 also saw the addition of a convertible to the Shelby line, which was available in both GT350 and GT500 form. However, with the advent of the more powerful 428 Cobra Jet engine, the GT500 became the GT500KR (King of the Road).

BELOW: Rocker panel stripes clearly identify the GT500KR, while the Cobra Jet emblem gives no doubt as to the type of engine used.

BELOW RIGHT: The Shelby Mustangs came to the end of the line with the '69-'70 models, which looked quite unlike the production Mustangs. They no longer offered significant performance gains over the standard high-performance Mustangs and so Ford allowed them to slip away.

Moreover, the Shelby now came in two body styles: the 2+2 fastback and the convertible. Suspension and running gear remained standard Mustang, although wider 15in. diameter tires and wheels produced handling gains.

In place of the GT350's 289 engine was the standard 302cu.in. V8 equipped with an aluminum inlet manifold and 600cfm Holley four-barrel carburetor. In this form, the engine developed 250bhp. The GT500 continued with the 428 engine, but with a single 650cfm Holley four-barrel and now rated at 360bhp. However, this engine was dropped part way through the year and replaced with the 428 Cobra Jet motor, whereupon the GT500 became the GT500KR (King of the Road). In a sense, it was 'King of the Road,' too, well at least as far as the Shelby stable was concerned; none of its stablemates could outrun a GT500KR, except maybe a 427-equipped GT500.

The Shelby Mustang received another new front end for 1969 that bore no resemblance to the standard car and there was even more liberal use of scoops and vents all round the body to change its appearance. The complete front end – fenders, front panel and hood – was in fiberglass and was much longer than the standard production car. A full-width grille opening was trimmed with chrome and contained a pair of headlights. The hood seemed to be full of scoops (in fact, three scoops and two vents), while additional scoops appeared in front of both front and rear wheel wells. The Thunderbird tail lights were retained, while the rear spoiler grew in size.

Once again fastback and convertible body styles were

chosen for the Shelby models, the running gear being essentially the same as the Mach 1. The GT350 received the 290bhp 351W engine with four-barrel carburetor and Ram Air, while the GT500 was equipped with the Ram Air version of the 428 Cobra Jet engine.

Not all of the 1969 models sold that year, so they were carried over and sold as 1970 models and with them the Shelby Mustang passed into history. Other than their unique body styling, by 1970 they had little to offer when compared to the performance versions of the standard Mustang.

Chapter 6

Mustang II: Back to Basics

When the Mustang II made its debut in 1974, it was clear that this was a completely new breed; it certainly had some familiar Mustang features, but it could no longer be considered a ponycar in the accepted sense of the term. Mustang II was a dumpy little car in the sub-compact league and it was short on horsepower. To even call the car a Mustang was a bit of an insult to all those enthusiasts who admired the original for its style and performance. Still, it met the need for a sporty-looking small car, as reflected in the sales figures, which were quite healthy.

Two body styles were offered: a fastback and a hardtop. They were based on a 96.2in. wheelbase with front and rear tracks of 55.6 and 55.8in. respectively. Overall length was 175in., overall width 70.2in. and height 50.3in. A few styling features provided a link with the Mustang of old; the grille opening was the same shape, contained parking lights and a running horse emblem and was flanked by separate headlights; there was a sculpted depression in each flank reminiscent of the earlier car's imitation brake cooling scoop. Otherwise, everything was new, and it wasn't all bad; the fastback Mustang II was now a hatchback, providing excellent access to the rear load area.

Beneath the skin was a new design of front suspension that held the springs between the upper and lower wishbones, while at the rear staggered shock absorbers were standard. Steering was rack and pinion and the front brakes were disks.

If potential Mustang II buyers were expecting traditional Mustang performance they would be disappointed, for the 1974 model was distinctly lacking in that department. As standard, the car came with a 140cu.in. overhead-cam four-cylinder engine that was a reworked version of the motor used in Ford's Pinto. Delivering 88bhp, this engine was severely taxed by the car's quite heavy weight (not far short of that of the original Mustang); even the optional 171cu.in. German-built overhead-valve V6, which developed 105bhp, could not produce sparkling performance (0-60mph in just under 14 seconds). A plus point was that both engines came with a four-speed manual gearbox as standard equipment, while a three-speed automatic was an option.

As with the original Mustang, the new car came with a comprehensive list of options, most of which were aimed at improving comfort and appearance rather than performance. There were two special models, too: the Ghia and the Mach 1. The Ghia was a luxury-trim version, based on the hardtop, that carried on from where the Grande left off, while the Mach 1 (fastback only) was mainly a cosmetic package, although it did come with the V6 engine and uprated suspension.

The Mustang II would retain the same basic body styling and engines throughout its production run, and most changes would be of a minor nature. However, in 1975 Ford did make an attempt to improve the rather dismal performance image of the car by making the 302cu.in. V8 available

ABOVE LEFT: When the new Mustang II arrived for 1974, it came as quite a shock. Although it had several Mustang styling clues, it certainly didn't have the sporty looks of the original as this hardtop shows.

LEFT: The running horse emblem was still there as were the headlights that flanked the grille, but somehow the package didn't quite work.

RIGHT: Two body styles were offered: a hardtop and a fastback, but both looked rather dumpy.

LEFT: There were very few major changes made throughout the life of the Mustang II, although one significant development was the availability of the 302cu.in. V8 that powers this Ghia hardtop. This model had been given opera windows in 1975.

RIGHT: The Cobra II was essentially a cosmetic package of spoilers and stripes, although it could be ordered with the 302. This one is a '78 model.

BELOW: The Ghia was the luxury model of the Mustang II herd and came about following Ford's purchase of the legendary Italian styling studio.

as an option. This was rated at 140bhp and came with the automatic transmission only. With this set-up, the car could sprint to 60mph in 10.5 seconds.

For those who wanted to match this performance with sporty looks, there was the Cobra II package that emulated the early Shelby Mustang. The Cobra II had front and rear spoilers, rear side window louvres, a hood scoop, custom wheels, bold striping and a Cobra emblem affixed to the grille. Inside were a sports steering wheel and brushed-aluminum trim panels. Sadly, the Cobra II pack didn't do a lot for the diminutive Mustang's already rather cluttered appearance.

For 1977, the hardtop could be ordered with an opening sunroof, while the fastback was given an optional T-top with removable roof panels. One benefit that year was that the 302 V8 could be had with a four-speed manual gearbox.

The last year of production for the Mustang II was 1978, and few changes were made. Ford did make one last attempt at giving the car a performance image, however, and succeeded in going way over the top. The King Cobra II was clearly inspired by Pontiac's Firebird Trans Am, but the aggressive-looking features of that low-slung monster did not translate too well to the dumpy little Mustang II. At the front, the car received a deep air dam, while there were flared rear wheel wells and a rear-mounted ducktail spoiler. On the hood was a rear-facing, non-functional scoop and a huge, stylized cobra decal.

Underneath the King Cobra's 'wolf' outfit was the 302 with four-speed, power-assisted steering and uprated suspension. It performed as well as any Mustang II had ever done, but it was all a far cry from the ground-pounding Mustang of old. Fortunately, yet another new breed of Mustang was about to be let out of the stable, one that would eventually uphold the reputation enjoyed by the original ponycar.

LEFT: The most outrageous-looking Mustang II was the King Cobra which came as standard with the 302 V8 and a four-speed manual transmission. It also had uprated suspension.

RIGHT: The King Cobra owed much of its styling to Pontiac's Firebird Trans Am, including that large cobra hood decal.

BELOW: The T-top, reversed hood scoop, spoilers and even rear wheelwell flares were all pure Trans Am, but the effect was of a sheep in wolf's clothing.

OFFICIAL PACE CAR
63rd. ANNUAL INDIANAPOLIS 500 MILE RACE MAY 27, 1979

Chapter 7
A New Beginning

Just as the Mustang II had been a surprise, so was the new Mustang for 1979. Although the engines of the old car were carried over, everything else was fresh and there were no longer any styling clues that provided a link with the past. Ford had started with a clean sheet of paper. Apart from the name, only the running horse emblem remained as a reminder of what had gone before.

Based on the Ford Fairmont floorpan, but with a shorter wheelbase at 100.4in., the new Mustang was given sleek, aerodynamic styling in two-door sedan and fastback form (the latter was a hatchback). The body was a full 4in. longer than the Mustang II, while front and rear track were both increased by 1in. The up-to-date design was to last well and is still the basis for the latest Mustangs to come out of Detroit.

The Mustang kept the 86bhp 140cu.in. ohc four-cylinder engine as standard, with the 105bhp V6 and 140bhp 302 V8 as options. Added to the optional engine range was a turbocharged version of the ohc four, which was rated at 132bhp and had been developed to provide V8 performance with the better fuel consumption of the four. Unfortunately, it would be a while before all the bugs were ironed out of this system; in the meantime, it gained a poor reputation. Four-speed manual gearboxes were standard with the four and six-cylinder engines, while the V8 came with a three-speed automatic.

Steering was still by rack and pinion, but the suspension design was all new. At the front were McPherson struts, but with the coil spring mounted between the lower wishbone and the chassis, and an anti-roll bar. The rear suspension comprised coil springs and telescopic shock absorbers with a four-link arrangement to locate the axle. An optional handling package was also available and comprised uprated springs and shock absorbers, front and rear anti-roll bars and Michelin TRX tires. The last were of an unusual size and required a set of special 5.9 × 15.4in. wheels.

Ford obviously still had some work to do with the new Mustang, for under hard acceleration the rear axles of V8-equipped cars suffered considerable axle tramp. Even so, they could reach 60mph in around 9 seconds.

As before a luxury Ghia model was made available (in both body styles) together with a performance version – the Cobra. The latter option was only available on the fastback and included as standard the turbocharged ohc four engine and the handling package. A large cobra hood decal, reminiscent of that used on the Mustang II King Cobra, was an option.

Another special model for 1979 was the Pace Car replica, intended to celebrate the Mustang's use as the official pace car for that year's Indianapolis 500 race. Finished in a two-tone paint scheme of silver-gray and black, the Pace Car

ABOVE LEFT: Ford's third generation Mustang was chosen to pace the 1979 Indianapolis 500 race and to commemorate that honor, the company offered the Pace Car replica. All had a silver-gray and black paint scheme and came with Pace Car decals for owners to add if they wished.

LEFT: One thing for sure, the 1979 Mustang was completely up to date in its styling. Both fastback and two-door sedan body styles were made.

RIGHT: There were no really obvious visual links with previous Mustangs, but a discreet hood badge carried the running horse emblem.

replica featured front and rear spoilers, a non-functional, rear-facing hood scoop, a sunroof and Recaro seats. The engine could be either the turbo four or the 302 V8.

One event that year that did prove a direct link between the new Mustang and the original ponycar was the substitution of the old 200cu.in. inline six for the German-built V6, which was in short supply.

By 1981, there had been further revisions to the engine line-up: the 302 V8 had been replaced by a 119bhp downsized version of the 255cu.in., while the turbo four was dropped. However, that engine did make one more appearance in a special Mustang developed by McLaren. This car conveyed a performance image in no uncertain terms, having a massive hood scoop, substantial spoilers and heavily flared fenders. Uprated suspension and special wide wheels shod with Firestone HPR radials ensured excellent handling for this limited-edition road and trackster.

The 302 V8 returned for 1982 in the revived Mustang GT, which replaced the Cobra and came with front and rear spoilers, a hood scoop and the TRX handling package. To combat the inevitable tramp with this powerful engine, Ford installed a set of traction bars, which helped the car sprint to 60mph in less than 8 seconds. Both the 302 and the 255cu.in. V8s were options on all other models of the Mustang, which were now designated L, GL and GLX in ascending level of luxury. The Ghia was no more.

LEFT: In 1984, to celebrate the 20th anniversary of the Mustang, Ford issued the GT350, a limited-edition model that came with the 302 V8 or turbo four.

RIGHT: The 302 V8 used in the 1984 GT350; Ford were now quoting engine size in liters, hence the legend on the air cleaner.

BELOW LEFT: The 20th anniversary special carried rocker panel stripes and the GT350 designation just like the Shelby Mustangs of old, but it had absolutely nothing to do with Carroll Shelby.

BELOW: The GT350 was also available in convertible form. All GT350s were white with red stripes and interior.

OVERLEAF: Like its predecessors, the new Mustang convertible looked good with the top down.

G.T.350

MUSTANG
Ford
WANDER
17 S 372
INDIANA

ABOVE: By 1986 the front end of the Mustang had been restyled, much after the manner of the special Mustang SVO. This is a GT convertible.

LEFT: The Mustang SVO was built by Ford's Special Vehicle Operations division and was a sophisticated, high-performance car in the European mold.

ABOVE RIGHT: Although it doesn't have the sporty lines of the original Mustang, the third-generation car provides ponycar-type performance.

RIGHT: The '86 GT Mustang offered plenty of performance thanks to its 200bhp 302 V8 that was equipped with electronic fuel injection.

LEFT: The very functional dashboard of the '86 GT Mustang is very much like an aircraft's instrument panel.

BELOW: This 1987 GT fastback coupe has the modern high-performance look that gels really well with its overall styling. Functional spoilers, side skirts and louvered rear light covers all add to the appeal.

For 1983, the Mustang received mildly restyled front and rear ends and a convertible returned to the line-up for the first time in 10 years. By now, the Mustang was a serious rival to GM's Chevrolet Camaro and Pontiac Firebird, which had remained true to the ponycar concept from the very beginning. As a result, the accent began to shift more and more toward performance – just like in the old days.

The 302 was now made to pump out 175bhp through modifications to its breathing system and it was backed by a close-ratio five-speed gearbox, allowing the Mustang to reach 60mph in close on 6 seconds. Other changes to the engine range included the dropping of the 255cu.in. V8 and the inline six. In place of the latter was a new V6, this time displacing 232cu.in. and rated at 112bhp.

Continuing the performance theme, 1983 saw the introduction of the Turbo GT. This was equipped with the turbocharged four-cylinder engine, but instead of a carburetor, it featured electronic fuel injection which was much more efficient than the original set-up. In this form, the engine put out 145bhp.

Another version of the turbocharged four appeared in the limited-edition Mustang SVO of 1984, developed by Ford's Special Vehicle Operations division. This engine was reworked to produce 175bhp, the induction system incorporating an intercooler and tuned-port fuel injection. Other features of the SVO included a five-speed manual gearbox, Traction Lok limited-slip differential, four-wheel disk brakes, uprated suspension and 7 × 16in. aluminum wheels shod with Goodyear NCT tires.

The bodywork of the SVO was as distinctive as its running gear with a large hood scoop, double rear spoiler and special grille, while inside were adjustable seats and a leather-rimmed steering wheel. The SVO was an impressive package in the European mold, offering excellent handling and performance (0-60 in around 7.5 seconds), but in many ways it was too sophisticated – and too expensive when compared to the GT.

Ford celebrated the Mustang's 20th anniversary in 1984 by issuing a limited-edition GT model under the designation GT350, which hadn't been used since the last Shelby

LEFT: Part of the package with the '87 GT was this large rear wing. The louvered light covers are a unique touch.

RIGHT: Later versions of the 302 V8 came with this electronically-controlled fuel injection unit.

BELOW RIGHT: The Mustang has come a long way since 1964. In 1990, Ford introduced this 5.0 model. Its sleek, elegant lines are typical of the company's modern design ethic.

Mustang left the corral in 1970. The GT350 could be either a fastback or a convertible with the high-performance 302 V8 or the turbo GT four. All came in white with special stripes and lettering, while inside SVO-style seats were a feature of the all-red interior.

Another newcomer for '84 was a 165bhp version of the 302 V8 with throttle-body fuel injection. This was intended for use with the automatic transmission.

Further engine improvements to the 302 in 1985 saw the high-performance version producing 210bhp. Among the changes were a camshaft with roller lifters and a new dual exhaust system incorporating tubular headers. The GT also received suspension changes to improve handling. These included new wheels and tires (as used on the SVO) and a quad-shock-absorber arrangement to help control rear axle tramp. All cars received the same front end treatment as the SVO model.

There were few changes in 1986, but 1987 saw a major restyling exercise with the front end being made much sleeker and incorporating flush-mounted headlights and wrap-around turn-signal lamps. Flush glass was fitted all round, while a new design of tail light was installed. This form would be the basis of all Mustangs to date.

Power of the 302 was increased to 225bhp (220bhp with the automatic transmission), while the ohc four received fuel injection as standard and jumped to 90bhp. It came with a five-speed manual gearbox or optional automatic. There was no V6 in the line-up.

The GT, which was supplied with the 302 V8, also had a package of body panels that certainly made it stand out. A front air dam, side skirts and rear spoiler, together with scoops ahead of the front and rear wheels made an impressive sight. The GT was an impressive performer, too, sprinting to 60mph in under six seconds and being capable of reaching almost 150mph. Although the style was different, the Mustang had become a true ponycar once more.

Since then there have been few changes to his new breed of Mustang. However, its long production run would seem to suggest that the next chapter in the story is about to unfold. Keep your eye on the stable door.

ABOVE: The beautiful, low-slung elegance of the 1993 Ford Mustang Mach III.

LEFT: Prominently displaying its Mustang badge, this 1993 Cobra has been captured cornering at speed.

Index

Page numbers in *italics* refer to illustrations

ACKNOWLEDGMENTS

The author and publisher would like to thank David Eldred for designing this book, Stephen Small for the picture research and Ron Watson for the index. The following individuals and agencies provided photographic material:

Brompton Books, pages: 2-3(Nicky Wright), 9(both/Nicky Wright), 10(both/Nicky Wright), 11(top/Nicky Wright), 12(bottom/Nicky Wright), 13(top), 14(top/Nicky Wright), 15(bottom/Nicky Wright), 16-17(Nicky Wright), 20(bottom/Nicky Wright), 21(both/Nicky Wright), 24(both/Nicky Wright),26(top/Nicky Wright), 27(bottom/Nicky Wright), 28(top/Nicky Wright), 29(top/Nicky Wright), 30(Nicky Wright), 32(bottom/Nicky Wright), 33(bottom/Nicky Wright), 34(both/Nicky Wright), 36(both/Nicky Wright), 36(both/Nicky Wright), 52(bottom/Nicky Wright), 53(Nicky Wright), 54(Nicky Wright), 55(both/Nicky Wright), 56(both/Nicky Wright),, 60(both/Nicky Wright), 61(top/Nicky Wright), 64(top/Nicky Wright), 65(both/Nicky Wright), 66(top/Nicky Wright), 69(top/Nicky Wright), 70(top/Nicky Wright).

Neill Bruce, pages: 42(both/Tobjorn Hansson), 43(Tobjorn Hansson), 44-45 (all four/Tobjorn Hansson), 46(both/Tobjorn Hansson), 58(bottom/Peter Roberts, 59(Peter Roberts), 64(bottom/Nicky Wright), 70(both).

Colin Burnham, pages: 4-5, 16(bottom), 17(top).

National Motor Museum, England, pages: 1, 6-7(Nicky Wright), 8(both/Nicky Wright), 11(bottom/Nicky Wright), 12(top/Nicky Wright), 15(top), 17(bottom), 18(both/Nicky Wright), 20(top), 22(Nicky Wright), 23(Nicky Wright), 25(both/Nicky Wright), 26(bottom/Nicky Wright), 29(bottom/Nicky Wright), 31(both/Nicky Wright), 32(top/Nicky Wright), 35(Nicky Wright), 37(both/Nicky Wright), 38(Nicky Wright), 39(Nicky Wright), 40-41(Nicky Wright), 47(both, 48-49, 50(top), 50(bottom/Nicky Wright), 51(top/Nicky Wright), 51(bottom), 52(top/Nicky Wright), 57(Nicky Wright), 58(top/Nicky Wright), 61(bottom/Nicky Wright), 62-63(Nicky Wright), 66-67(Nicky Wright), 68(Nicky Wright), 69(bottom/Nicky Wright).